D1505045

# Gifts for Gus

## The Sound of Hard G

By Peg Ballard

# Gus got a lot of gifts.

# Gus got a toy car.

5

6

# Gus got a goldfish.

Gus got
a wagon.

10

# Gus got a book.

# Gus got
# a green ball.

**13**

Gus got
new boots.

15

# Gus got gumballs.

17

18

# Gus got a gold hat.

# Gus got many good gifts.

21

# Word List:

| | |
|---|---|
| gifts | green |
| gold | gumballs |
| goldfish | Gus |
| good | wagon |
| got | |

# Note to Parents and Educators

The books in this series are based on current research, which supports the idea that our brains are pattern-detectors rather than rules-appliers. This means children learn to read easier when they are taught the familiar spelling patterns found in English. As children encounter more complex words, they have greater success in figuring out these words by using the spelling patterns.

Throughout the series, the texts provide the reader with the opportunity to practice and apply knowledge of the sounds in natural language. The books introduce sounds using familiar onsets and *rimes,* or spelling patterns, for reinforcement.

For example, the word *cat* might be used to present the short "a" sound, with the letter *c* being the onset and "_at" being the rime. This approach provides practice and reinforcement of the short "a" sound, as there are many familiar words made with the "_at" rime.

The stories and accompanying photographs in this series are based on time-honored concepts in children's literature: well-written, engaging texts and colorful, high-quality photographs combine to produce books that children want to read again and again.

Dr. Peg Ballard
Minnesota State University, Mankato

**The Child's World®**
childsworld.com

Published by The Child's World®
1980 Lookout Drive • Mankato, MN 56003-1705
800-599-READ • www.childsworld.com

**ACKNOWLEDGMENTS**
The Child's World®: Mary Swensen, Publishing Director
The Design Lab: Design
Michael Miller: Editing

**PHOTO CREDITS**
© Hurst Photo/Shutterstock.com: 9; Jami Garrison/
Shutterstock.com: 17; Johanna Goodyear/Shutterstock.
com: 6; kongsky/Shutterstock.com: 18; Quang Ho/
Shutterstock.com: cover; Supertrooper/Shutterstock.com:
14; suriya yapin/Shutterstock.com: 13; Tatiana Popova/
Shutterstock.com: 5; vitaliy_73/Shutterstock.com: 10;
wavebreakmedia/Shutterstock.com: 2, 21

ISBN 9781503809215
LCCN 2015958474

Printed in the United States of America
Mankato, MN
June, 2016
PA02310

## ABOUT THE AUTHOR

Dr. Peg Ballard holds a PhD from Purdue
University and is an associate professor
in the Department of Elementary & Early
Childhood Education at Minnesota State
University, Mankato. Her areas of expertise
are assessment, interventions, and
response to intervention. Dr. Ballard teaches
online graduate courses in the K–12 reading
licensure and master's program along with
reading interventions in the undergraduate
teacher preparation program.